Practical Poetry

R. K. Dawson

To all my good friends at Southgate. Best wishes to all.

Ron Dawson

12-26-96

VANTAGE PRESS
New York

To my wife, Sherry, my son, Chris, my daughter, Michele, my
grandson, Aaron, and my granddaughter, Crystal

3 9082 06559999 8

FIRST EDITION

Copyright © 1994 by R. K. Dawson

Published by Vantage Press, Inc.
516 West 34th Street, New York, New York 10001

Manufactured in the United States of America
ISBN: 0-533-10815-2

0 9 8 7 6 5 4 3 2 1

Contents

Introduction

Reap the knowledge as you read the lines,
For the poetry that follows and all its rhymes.

Imagine being in a green forest among the tall pines,
Or hearing the singing birds, so many kinds.

Capture the moment as you read this book with its poetic
    lines,
Read the passages of the different poems that touch your
    minds.

May you enjoy this book today and forever, forever, forever.

Dinosaurs

The name dinosaur means "terrible lizard," and they roamed
the earth about 65 million years ago; their name is no *more*.
We know about the different kinds of these great reptiles
because their bones and teeth are found as fossils throughout
every land and *shore*.

Dinosaurs were all reptiles and had leathery or scaly skin.
Their young hatched from eggs with shells. Some dinosaurs
were small while others were enormous. They frightened
most other animals on *sight*.
Some dinousaurs were plant eaters, others were meat eaters
and when they met, there was usually a terrible *fight*.

The Iguanodon was a plant eater who had no front teeth, but
he had a hard *beak*.
Plants, flowers, leaves, and stems he would *seek*.
He also had sharp eyes and ears and a hooklike finger on his
hand.
The Iguanodon was about thirty-three feet long and weighed
about three tons. He walked on his back legs through the
forest and *sand*.

Plateosaurus was the first of the large plant-eating
dinosaurs; he had a very long *tail*.
He ate leaves and plants with his small teeth and reached up
to the top of the trees to eat without *fail*.
He was over twenty-eight feet long and was twenty feet *tall*.
As he hit his enemies with his powerful body, he would watch
them *fall*.

Triceratops was also a plant-eater and had three horns on his
head shield. His name means "three-horn face." He had a
strong neck plate, numerous teeth, and had a mouth like a
hooked *beak*.

1

They weighed seven tons, and were thirty feet long, and traveled in herds through the green forest. Leaves, plants, stems, and shoots they would *seek*.

Stegosaurus had three-foot spikes on its tail. He was twenty-three feet long and had large bony plates on his *back*. He weighed one and a half tons, had short powerful legs, but courage he did not *lack*.
He ate leaves, flowers, and plants. He moved about very *slowly*.
His enemies he kept at bay with his powerful tail and would force them to *go*.

Tyrannosaurus is named "tyrant lizard" and was the most feared meat-eating dinosaur. He had a powerful body, weighed seven tons, and was forty-six feet tall. He also had frightening six-inch teeth. He would attack his prey with ease. Tyrannosaurus was the king of the dinosaurs and also was the biggest flesh-eating land creature *ever*.
Will there ever be another creature like him? No, *never*.

There were many, many other dinosaurs that roamed the earth so long *ago*.
Were the dinosaurs wiped out by meteorites or by the blotting out of the sun? Did this cause severe weather changes?
Scientists have many other questions on why the dinosaurs became extinct. It must have been quite a *show*.
At the beginning, the age of the dinosaurs must have been a sight to see, a new era of *revitalization*.
That is all gone now, but no one will really know what caused their *obliteration*.

Country

The opening eyelids of the morn appear,
The start of another day is now here.

The sun shines down on the country below,
As nature begins her glamorous show.

See the shadows on the rolling hills
Gaze upon the meadows and the daffodils.

The clouds move across the blue sky,
As the birds leave their nests and begin to fly.

Animals are put to pasture for the long day,
One can also see the trees as they begin to sway.

The woods are filled with living things,
What beauty their romp and movement brings.

The blazing sun heats the earth and makes everything grow,
The grass, flowers, plants, and trees begin to show.

The hay in the meadow casts a golden hue upon the sand,
The whole country is alive and vibrant as one views this great
    land.

The crickets start chirping their favorite song,
As everything in the forest keeps moving along.

The day is ending as the sun begins to fade,
The trees and hills are barely seen in the shade.

The Empress of Silence and the Queen of Sleep appear,
Awaiting tomorrow, tomorrow, tomorrow.

The European Community

The last verse of Daniel in chapter seven speaks of the beast
that has ten *horns*.
Could the European Community be the beast that the Bible
forewarns?

The current E.C. members are twelve. They are Belgium,
Britain, Denmark, Germany, Greece, Ireland, Italy,
Luxemburg, The Netherlands, Portugal, Spain, and *France*.
Which two countries will drop out and which will remain? Is
this by *chance*?

The Maastricht treaty of the E.C. calls for an accord for
common foreign and security policies, a joint central bank,
and a single currency by *1999*.
This is a rebirth of the Roman Empire. One world
government, one world economy, and one world religion. Is
this another *sign*?

The Roman Empire was also led by ten nations. With this
revival, the Antichrist will appear from one of the ten E.C.
countries and make a treaty with Israel, and there will be
peace.
The hunger of the people, world and civil wars will appear to
cease.

As told in the Bible, another little horn will spring up from
the ten horns and destroy all that are against the beast. The
world will be *terrified*.
Some of the prophecies of Daniel reveal the signs of the
present time. An army of 200 million advancing from the
East. China now has that number. An army will cross the
Euphrates River on dry land. In 1990 Turkey built a dam in
fulfillment of this prophecy. We have seen famine, plagues,
earthquakes, a falling away of the churches, weather

4

changes, communism, dictatorship, collapse of family values, and world wars. The people of the world will be *petrified*.

Beware of the ten kings of the E.C. and what they represent. Only when these events occur will God and His angels *intervene*. The forces of Heaven will overcome the beast. Be prepared. Pray to God as He defeats the devil in that terrible *scene*.

Father Time

Birthdays come and go; they say that birthdays are for the
    young, not the old.
The impression is that age is just a number, I'm told.

Ah, youth! The spirit of life is like a flower of age.
As a person matures, Father Time takes over with a rage.

The birthdays continue as I celebrate them year after year.
The passage of time goes on, a time that will never come
back and the memories become so dear.

Although they are happy days, the minutes, hours, and days
    pass,
Are those wrinkles on my face as I gaze into the glass?

Middle age arrives, along with the aches and pains. Why do I
    feel
like I've been on a rack?
After all, I'm in good shape,
but why do I have a sore back?

The fountain of my youth is gone now
as I arrive at the autumn of my years.
The corridors of time have taken their toll
and have eased my many tears.

As the span of life reaches a new era,
I reflect on the years gone by, for time flies.
At another day or another hour
I'll say my good-byes.

The Emerald Forest

As you walk into my green forest, notice my many trees. The giant oak, birch, chestnut, elm, black walnut, and spruce. See my multicolored ferns growing on the forest floor. Look up at the tall pine trees.

Continue on through my forest as you tread upon the soft floor of dead leaves and pine needles. Gaze upon my many plants, my olive green vines. See the blossoms of the wildflowers and their vivid colors.

As you pace yourself deeper into my woods, soon you will hear the gush of the flowing waters of my brooks and streams. Look closely in the clear cool water and watch my fish. The elusive brown trout, brook trout, and the speckled trout.

Sit upon a tree stump and watch; be quiet and still. Listen and look. See my many birds. The partridge, cardinal, bluejay, crow, and other species of hawks and owls. Watch the fleet-footed, white-tailed deer, squirrels, chipmunks, groundhogs, woodchucks, rabbits, turkeys, and porcupines.

As you leave my great cathedral, walk slowly, slowly out and wonder at what you have seen, and always remember the beauty of my Emerald Forest.

The Rose of Autumn

A rose is a rose, is a rose,
Its sensuous smell is like fine prose.

The dark velvet colors are soft yet are bright,
As the morning dew sets on the roses in the light.

The sun shines brightly on the buds and flowers,
As the rose bursts open, one sees God's wondrous powers.

The final rose of autumn is here,
Showing its beauty for the final time this year.

A Rainy Day

If you want it to rain, name a location,
or simply go on vacation.

The clouds are dreary and the skies are gray,
the rain falls down steadily all day.

Instead of the opening eyelids of the morn,
I saw the fine mist of rain being born.

Noontime showed no promise of the sun to appear,
Water, water everywhere was apparent, I fear.

The birds outside were chirping their gallant bliss,
as the rain fell quietly in a fine mist.

Nighttime approaches, the Empress of Silence and the
Queen of Sleep appear, awaiting tomorrow, tomorrow,
tomorrow.

Summer Flowers

Gaze upon my flowers to brighten up your day,
The white and yellow daisies make a beautiful bouquet.

The powder baby-blue wildflowers are swell,
as you breathe in the scent of their sweet smell.

The golden wildflowers show their wondrous face,
the work of art sits on the table
with the picturesque flowers in the vase.

Cast your eyes upon the view, look and see,
as you see the pretty flowers, think of me.

The flowers bring peace, like the pureness of a dove,
Have a good day and enjoy the bouquet, my love.

Aaron

Aaron is our grandson, a bundle of joy,
He runs, plays, and laughs, what a boy.

His big blue eyes shine over his face,
He walks, crawls, and climbs all over the place.

Aaron loves the water, especially his bath,
He plays with his toys with a big laugh.

He sits on my lap with his book in hand,
As he looks and points at the pictures, isn't that grand?

He likes TV cartoons and loves anything sweet,
He gives a hug and kiss that can't be beat.

Grandma rocks him to sleep with tender loving care,
As she sings and strokes his blond hair.

Grandma and Grandpa count their blessings and give him
      our love,
For the little angel whom God has sent us from above.

The "terrible twos" are not so bad, you see,
Not when we have a grandson as cute as can be.

Will we ever give up our Aaron? Never.
For he is ours to love forever, forever, forever.

Summer

The soft summer breeze blows across the blue sky,
The clouds form shapes as they go by.

Children everywhere are laughing and playing in the sun,
They romp and play in their make-believe world, having fun.

Flowers are in full bloom showing their colorful bed,
They make a pretty arrangment around the shed.

Birds are chirping and serenading the trees,
You can hear their songs and melodies.

Plants and shrubs are a vibrant green,
The grass as well is a welcome sight to be seen.

Kids are splashing in the pool,
As they play their games and try to stay cool.

Barbecues and picnics are the times of the season,
As people cherish these activities with good reason.

The lazy-hazy days of summer are here, it can't be beat,
Enjoy this time and the summer heat.

Freedom

What we Americans call freedom is now a reality over most of
the sphere.
The people of the world rebel as they gather to claim their
rights, but they do so in fear.

Many hardships have been made by the people of various
countries in the East;
Germany, Poland, Hungary, and Czechoslovakia fight for
freedom yet celebrate with a feast.

You hear their cries of reconstruction in government and
economic reform;
The breakaway from communism continues as the newly
elected leaders perform.

The people want jobs, housing, and enough food to eat;
The complicated task is now beginning as world leaders meet.

The wall of communism has come down as the people
continue their fight.
They pray to God for help, but it will be many years before
freedom is in sight.

The Russian people also continue their struggle for a free
land;
The long bread lines and the high prices for food go on as the
people fight for a free hand.

Independence, self-government, and freedom will be won by
all;
Communist countries can no longer restrain the people in
their quest for liberty and justice; the countries will fall.

The Ancient Women

The woman in white has appeared to us many times over the
years;
She has warned us, the human race, that sins against God
have caused her many fears.

The three young ones at Fatima were told by her of the things
to come;
The visions warn us of the terrible things that will happen to
the world, yet her warnings are heeded by some.

The three prophecies revealed to the three children were of
great horror, it makes one shake;
The King's Mother cries as tears fall down her cheeks; is she
telling us of Armageddon, or the coming of the great quake?

The Ancient Woman has appeared to us in hopes of
redeeming the world, to be better Christians and that sins
against God must cease;
We hope and pray that wars and famine across the world will
stop, as Mary, the Mother of God, pleads for peace.

The Rapture of Tchaikovsky

We praise the great music of the Russian composer, Pyotr
Tchaikovsky is his name;
The aftermath of his genius lies in his works of operas,
ballets, and symphonies, which brought him fame.

A deeply sensitive man, his romantic musicals were about
rural Russian countryside.
His divine passion for symphonies and ballets gave him great
pride.

He conducted concerts of great harmony and composition;
Once again his music was of his typical Russian tradition.

His *Swan Lake* and *Nutcracker* are the most popular ballets
today;
We delight in these musical scores and marvel at how well
the orchestra can play.

Tchaikovsky's music is world-renowned and will be enshrined
in the minds of men forever, forever, forever.

Valentine's Day

See the red clouds of the morn,
The start of another day is born.

What makes this day so special is you,
For all the things you say and do.

Gaze upon my flowers on this, your day;
You are special to me in every way.

I'm just wild about Sherry and she's just mad about me;
I hope this day is full of joy, be as happy as you can be.

As you savor the arrangement, enjoy what you see;
And as you look at the bouquet, think of me.

You and your heart are mine;
Won't you be my Valentine?

Desert Storm

The players are ready in the great arena, the stage is set,
President Bush has given the order to attack until victory is
     met.

We will end the Iraqis' occupation of Kuwait and end the war,
The reign of terror by Saddam Hussein will be no more.

The sorties continue to bomb Iraq's military sites day and
     night,
The likes of the Allied strikes have never been seen before;
They drive the enemy to fright.

Operation Desert Storm goes on with full force on Iraq's shore,
As the Army, Air Force, Navy, and Marines prepare for the
     land war.

All attempts to end the war have failed to bring peace,
Our men and women fight on until the battle will cease.

The full-scale battle was launched against Iraq in that place,
The enemy is defecting to the Allied forces and is losing face.

The war will linger on until Kuwait is liberated from Iraq,
Only then will all their land and possessions be given back.

The Allied flags will fly as peace is brought to this land,
The winds of war will settle as our troops arrive on the sand.

We support our troops in this desert war,
And wait for their return, to fight no more.

All honor and glory will be given to them as the war is put to
     rest,
Our men and women have shown the world that they are the
     best.

Now we see the end of the story,
As we capture the victory, we can see "Old Glory."

The blanket of peace covers the globe as our Allies unite,
We have beaten and devastated the enemy and won the fight.

Nostradamus's Prophecies

In the year 1999, wars, famine, and drought will spread,
The struggle for life will continue but leave many dead.

The clash of arms goes on, the mushroom clouds appear,
People all over the world run in terror and fear.

The gallant heroes fight on with great nerve and deeds.
Who are these cold-hearted foes that dare to destroy our
    seeds?

They come from the East, fast and furious across land and
    sea,
The Antichrist strikes as the holocaust causes many to flee.

People pray to God for divine intervention
To save them from their suffering and pain,
It will appear that their pleas go unanswered and many are
    slain.

Buildings fall, the earth quakes with destruction
As missiles come from space,
Plague, famine, and death are everywhere in that place.

The red hats from Rome flee as the fleet reaches its shore.
Is this to be the end of the Church, or is there more?

The Great King of Terror arrives
Among the slaughtered people to feast,
The Bible tells us that 666 is the number of the beast.

He shall rule over the world, this man of war,
The like of Satan has never been seen before.

Thirst and hunger will still rule over this trodden sod,
Before Christ comes to this land with His Holy Rod.

Satan will lose this great battle and go,
But the people of the world will still be filled with woe.

The powerful King arrives from the skies,
People everywhere weep, you can hear their cries,

The slaughter has ended as God works His wondrous plan,
Peace and prosperity rule the world in His domain and land.

Men, women, and children throughout the globe see His look,
The prophecies are now fulfilled as was written in the Good
    Book.

March Madness

Pump it up, move the ball, we have got to score,
We need the points; if we lose, there is no more.

Find the open man, pick the screen, and drive the lane,
Go for the three, get the win, and we will find fame.

The crowd is going wild as the score is tied once more,
The game is fast, but once more the defense "slams the door."

The opponent shoots, hits the rim,
The rebound is put in with yet another "stuff."
Our coach yells from the bench, now that's enough.

Pump it up, get going, another shot hits the glass,
Two more points for us; did you see that pass?

The two teams are tied with less than ten seconds to go,
We take a time out and we have the ball, what a show.

The pass is thrown to center court
As the guard shoots for the net,
The ball falls through the basket and our goal is met.

We made it to the Sweet Sixteen
And now advance to the Final Four for the last game,
The national championship is at stake,
We will never be the same.

Pump it up, it doesn't get any better than this,
With our great team and fans, we can't miss.

The Mountain

Gaze upon the majestic view of my peaks. See my icy slopes jutting from my sides. The snow covers my summit as the clouds go by. Gather your strength, your courage as you attempt to climb me. Many have tried, some have reached the top and planted their flags on my summit, other gallant men have perished.

You may climb upon my rock, but remember the lessons of those who were denied. Learn my secrets, my crevices as you try to reach my heights. Beware of the cold wind, the snow, and the blinding sun. Prepare yourself. Listen to the guides, for they know me. Be cautious, smart, listen, and travel slowly, slowly upon my icy black rock.

Stand firm in your commitment to ascend me, be positive in the treacherous task before you. As you reach my mountain crest, thank God for His help. Apply the lessons learned here to every day in your life as you finish today and await another task tomorrow.

Marlene's Grandchildren

The children are all happy as can be,
First there is green-eyed Jensey, she is three.

Then comes Ashley, who is five, and has eyes of blue,
She always asks Grandma why and what should she do?

Next of the girls is Lindsey, a cute little girl of six,
She is always teasing everyone with her little tricks.

Finally there is Kyle, a bright two-year-old boy,
The "terrible twos" have arrived but he is still Grandma's joy.

Three girls against one boy doesn't seem fair,
But Marlene gives them all her tender, loving care.

They are mischievous as they romp and play,
And they all laugh and giggle throughout the day.

Marlene takes them shopping and buys them pretty things,
And is delighted to watch and see what their happiness
    brings.

She knows their cheerfulness gives her joy and bliss,
She loves everyone and gives them all a big hug and kiss.

Grandchildren are special and Marlene is well aware
that the children will grow up fast,
So she must capture the moment while the time will last.

Her love for the children will be continuous as the stars that
    shine,
As she proudly says that "These grandchildren are mine."

Carie

All about Carie, there's so much to tell,
She is my neighbor gal and also my pal.

Slender and slim with long brown hair,
She is tall, pretty, and her complexion is fair.

Carie is spoiled, but she is a strong-willed girl,
Her personality sparkles like a precious pearl.

As you gaze into her eyes, be wary,
Her looks are deceptive, that's Carie.

Born under the sign of Aries
Over the years I watched her grow,
From babe to a beautiful young lady, her looks show.

Carie is always laughing,
My memories of her will last for quite a while,
Our friendship will last forever
Regardless of where she goes
And I'll keep remembering her smile.

The Ghosts of the Sea

The ghosts of the sunken ships remember the fog,
It was like the danger of a wild, mad dog.

Hidden in the darkness it came into the night,
Everyone aboard the sailing ship became afright.

They lost their way in that thick cloud
As they felt the rhythm of the waves,
They could hear the water
As it crashed against the shore and caves.

Before the sailors knew it
They were in the sea among the rolling, foaming crests,
The deep sea was calling them
As the waves broke across their breasts.

The high seas had taken another ship as it lay battered
among the rocks, moving slowly with the tide;
Softly they could hear the whispering of the fog as it
spoke to the ocean wide.

The ghosts of the sea beckon
As the ocean becomes a sheet of glass,
The fog has lifted and the ghosts of the deep
Invite the ships that would dare pass.